Bilingual Picture Dictionaries

My First Book of
Polish Words

by Katy R. Kudela

Translator: Translations.com

apple
jabłko
(YAHP-koh)

CAPSTONE PRESS
a capstone imprint

Table of Contents

How to Use This Dictionary

This book is full of useful words in both Polish and English. The English word appears first, followed by the Polish word. Look below each Polish word for help to sound it out. Try reading the words aloud.

Topic Heading in English

Word in English
Word in Polish
(pronunciation)

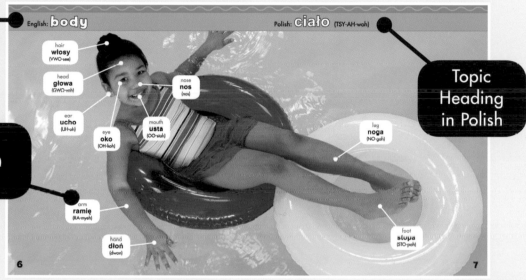

Topic Heading in Polish

English: **body**　　　　　　　　Polish: **ciało** (TSY-AH-woh)

hair
włosy
(VWO-see)

head
głowa
(GWO-vnh)

nose
nos
(nos)

ear
ucho
(UH-oh)

eye
oko
(OH-koh)

mouth
usta
(OO-stah)

leg
noga
(NO-gah)

arm
ramię
(RA-myeh)

hand
dłoń
(dwon)

foot
stopa
(STO-pah)

6　　　　　　　　　　7

Notes about the Polish Language

The Polish language uses the same alphabet as English, but there are a few letters with accent marks. These letters include: ą, ć, ę, ł, ń, ó, ś, and ż. To read the Polish letters, look at the pronunciation. The pronunciations can be read like English.

In many pronunciations, the letter "h" is added after a vowel. The "h" is to show a reader that the vowel can be read like English, such as "ah" for "a" and "oh" for "o."

In Polish, some letters are pronounced differently depending upon where they are used. Listed below are examples of some of these sounds.

ch = same as the letter "h"

cz = hard "ch" sound as in "church," "cheese," or "chicken"

dz = as in "reD Zone"

dz followed by an "i" = "j" as in "jeep"

rz = hard "sh" sound

sz = "sh" sound as in "shirt" or "shoes"

szcz = combination of both as the "shch" as in "freSH CHeese"

3

uncle
wujek
(VOO-yehk)

cousin
kuzyn
(KOO-zeen)

mother
mama
(MAH-mah)

aunt
ciotka
(TSY-OT-kah)

baby
niemowlę
(nye-MO-vleh)

Polish: rodzina (ro-DJEE-nah)

grandmother
babcia
(BAB-tsy-ah)

father
tata
(TAH-tah)

grandfather
dziadek
(DZYA-deck)

brother
brat
(braht)

sister
siostra
(SYO-strah)

5

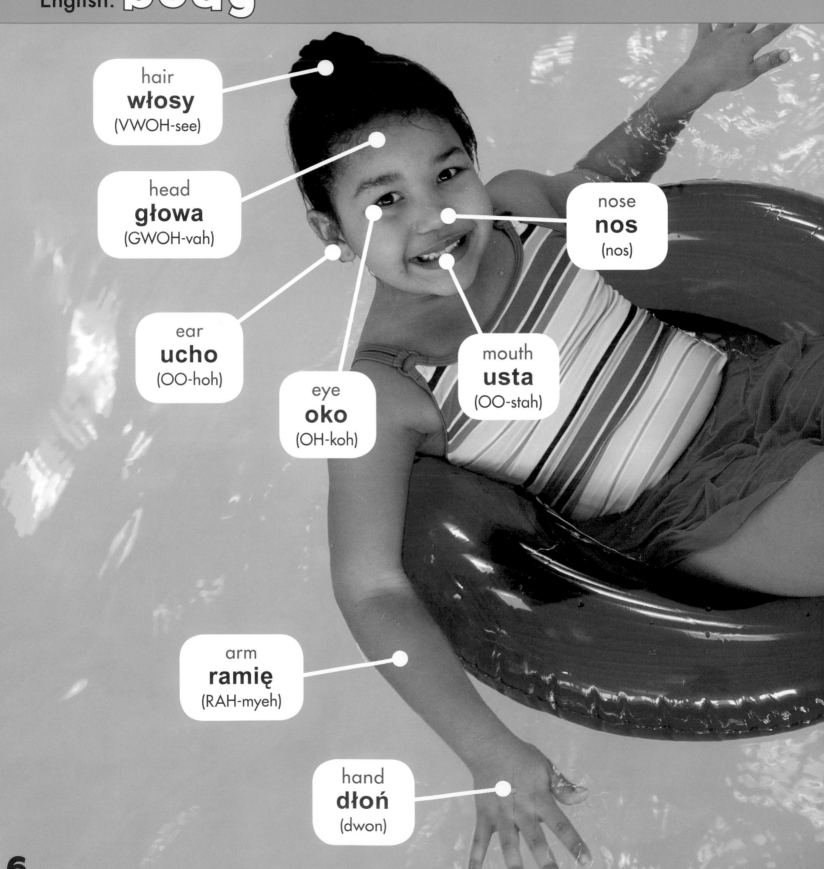

hair
włosy
(VWOH-see)

head
głowa
(GWOH-vah)

nose
nos
(nos)

ear
ucho
(OO-hoh)

mouth
usta
(OO-stah)

eye
oko
(OH-koh)

arm
ramię
(RAH-myeh)

hand
dłoń
(dwon)

leg
noga
(NOH-gah)

foot
stopa
(STOH-pah)

pajamas
piżama
(pee-JA-mah)

coat
kurtka
(KOOR-tkah)

shorts
szorty
(SHOR-tee)

boot
kalosz
(KAH-losh)

8

shoe
but
(boot)

hat
czapka
(CHAP-kah)

pants
spodnie
(SPOH-dnyeh)

sock
skarpeta
(skar-PEH-tah)

dress
sukienka
(soo-KYEN-kah)

shirt
koszula
(koh-SHOO-lah)

9

kite
latawiec
(lah-TAH-vyets)

doll
lalka
(LAL-kah)

puzzle
puzzle
(POOZ-leh)

train
pociąg
(POH-chyong)

wagon
wózek
(WOO-zehk)

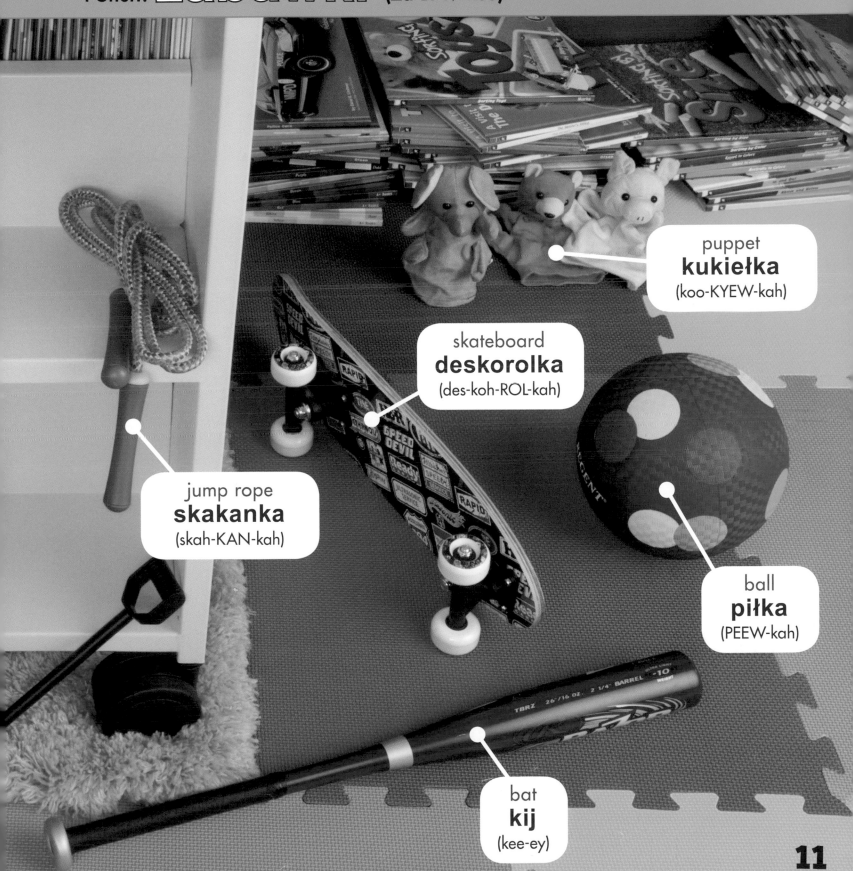

puppet
kukiełka
(koo-KYEW-kah)

skateboard
deskorolka
(des-koh-ROL-kah)

jump rope
skakanka
(skah-KAN-kah)

ball
piłka
(PEEW-kah)

bat
kij
(kee-ey)

11

window
okno
(OK-noh)

picture
obraz
(OB-rahz)

lamp
lampa
(LAM-pah)

dresser
komoda
(koh-MOH-dah)

curtain
zasłona
(zas-WOH-nah)

blanket
koc
(kohts)

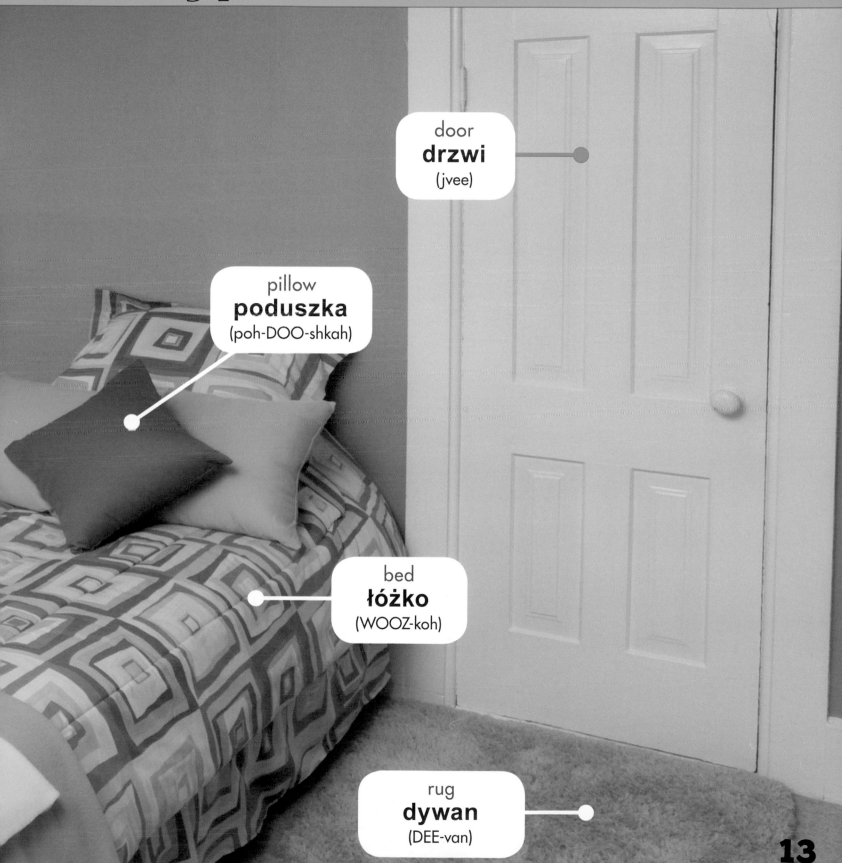

Polish: **sypialnia** (see-PYAL-nyah)

door
drzwi
(jvee)

pillow
poduszka
(poh-DOO-shkah)

bed
łóżko
(WOOZ-koh)

rug
dywan
(DEE-van)

13

bathtub
wanna
(VAN-nah)

soap
mydło
(MEED-woh)

toilet
muszla
(MOOSH-lah)

14

Polish: **łazienka** (wa-ZHYEN-kah)

toothbrush
szczoteczka do zębów
(shchoh-TETSH-kah doh ZEM-boof)

mirror
lustro
(loo-stroh)

toothpaste
pasta do zębów
(PAH-stah doh ZEM-boof)

comb
grzebień
(GSHEH-byenh)

sink
umywalka
(oo-mee-VAL-kah)

towel
ręcznik
(RENCH-neek)

brush
szczotka do włosów
(SHCHOT-kah doh VWOH-soof)

bowl
miska
(MEES-kah)

stove
kuchenka
(koo-HEN-kah)

pot
garnek
(GAHR-nehk)

oven
piec
(pyets)

refrigerator
lodówka
(loh-DOOF-kah)

knife
nóż
(noosh)

table
stół
(stoow)

plate
talerz
(TAH-lesh)

spoon
łyżka
(WEESH-kah)

fork
widelec
(vee-DEH-lets)

milk
mleko
(MLEH-koh)

carrot
marchewka
(mahr-HEF-kah)

bread
chleb
(hlep)

apple
jabłko
(YAHP-koh)

butter
masło
(MAS-woh)

egg
jajko
(YUY-koh)

pea
groszek
(GROH-shek)

orange
pomarańcza
(poh-mah-RAN-chah)

sandwich
kanapka
(kah-NAP-kah)

rice
ryż
(rish)

tractor
traktor
(TRAC-tor)

hay
siano
(SHYA-noh)

fence
płot
(pwot)

farmer
rolnik
(ROL-nick)

sheep
owca
(OF-cah)

pig
świnia
(SHVEE-nyah)

horse
koń
(kohn)

barn
stodoła
(stoh-DOH-wah)

cow
krowa
(KROH-vah)

chicken
kurczak
(KOOR-chuck)

leaf
liść
(leeshch)

butterfly
motyl
(MOH-teel)

flower
kwiat
(KVEE-yaht)

shovel
łopata
(woh-PAH-tah)

bird
ptak
(ptahk)

worm
dżdżownica
(jov-NEE-tsah)

22

plant
roślina
(roh-SHLEE-nah)

grass
trawa
(TRAH-vah)

dirt
ziemia
(ZYEH-myah)

seed
ziarno
(ZYAR-noh)

Edamame Green Soybean
Tohya
Glycine max

$2.99
Net Weight
15 grams
80 days
Warm season
crop - plant after
last chance of
spring frost

So high in
protein, it is
called "the meat
without bones".
Boiled, beans
are popped out
of the pod into
your mouth for
a culinary
delight!

23

brown
brązowy
(bron-ZO-veeh)

purple
fioletowy
(fyo-leh-TOH-vee)

orange
pomarańczowy
(poh-mah-ran-CHO-vee)

white
biały
(BYA-weeh)

red
czerwony
(cher-VOH-nee)

black
czarny
(CHAR-nee)

24

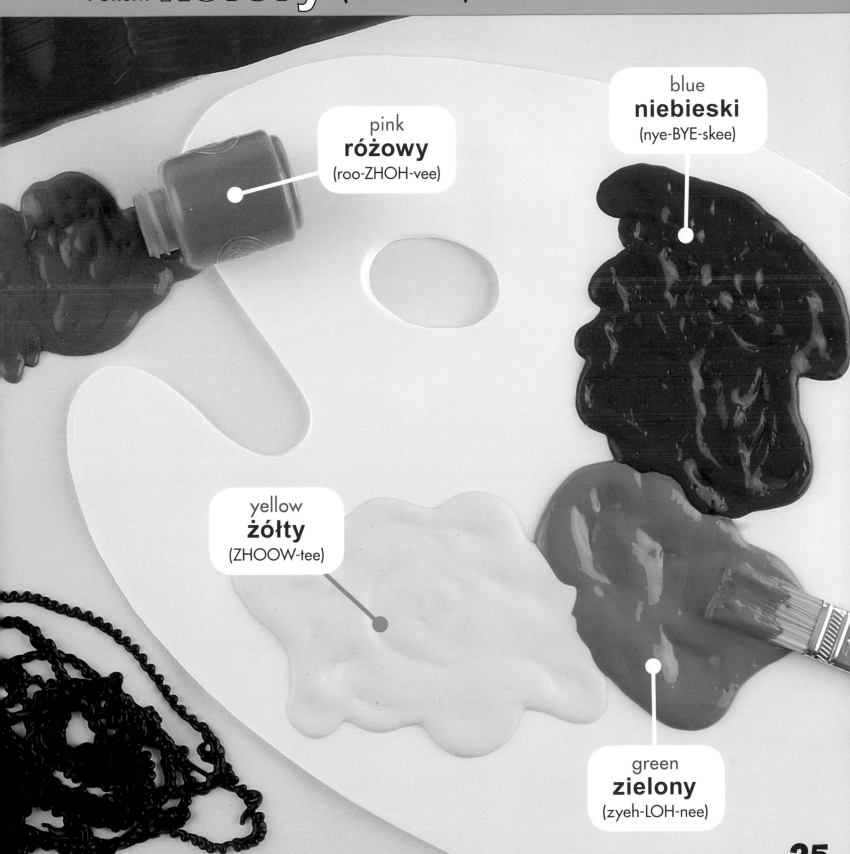

pink
różowy
(roo-ZHOH-vee)

blue
niebieski
(nye-BYE-skee)

yellow
żółty
(ZHOOW-tee)

green
zielony
(zyeh-LOH-nee)

teacher
nauczyciel
(nah-oo-CHEE-tchel)

book
książka
(KSHY-ONSH-kah)

desk
biurko
(BYOOR-koh)

pencil
ołówek
(oh-WOO-vek)

crayon
kredka
(KRET-kah)

clock
zegar
(ZEH-gahr)

map
mapa
(MAH-pah)

computer
komputer
(com-PU-ter)

chair
krzesło
(KSHE-swoh)

paper
papier
(PAH-pyer)

traffic light
światła
(SHVYA-tlah)

library
biblioteka
(bee-blyo-TEH-kah)

store
sklep
(sklep)

LIBRARY

ONE WAY

Tuesday 2:00-5:00
Thursday 2:00-6:00

bicycle
rower
(ROH-ver)

car
samochód
(sah-MOH-hood)

tree
drzewo
(JEH-voh)

bus
autobus
(auw-TOH-boos)

park
park
(park)

street
ulica
(OO-LEE-tsa)

sign
znak
(znahk)

STOP

29

Numbers • Liczby (LEETCH-bee)

1. one • **jeden** (YEH-dehn)
2. two • **dwa** (dvah)
3. three • **trzy** (tshee)
4. four • **cztery** (CHTEH-ree)
5. five • **pięć** (pyentsh)

6. six • **sześć** (sheshch)
7. seven • **siedem** (SYEH-dehm)
8. eight • **osiem** (OH-syem)
9. nine • **dziewięć** (DSJEH-vyehntsh)
10. ten • **dziesięć** (DSJEH-syehntsh)

Useful Phrases • Przydatne zwroty (pshee-DAT-neh ZVRO-tee)

yes • **tak** (takh)

no • **nie** (nyeh)

hello • **cześć** (tcheshch)

good-bye • **do widzenia** (doh vi-DSEN-ee-ah)

good morning • **dzień dobry** (djen DOH-bree)

good night • **dobranoc** (do-BRAH-nots)

please • **proszę** (PROH-sheh)

thank you • **dziękuję** (djen-KOO-yah)

excuse me • **przepraszam** (pshe-PRAH-sham)

My name is _____. • **Nazywam się** _____. (nah-ZI-vahm syeh)

Read More

Amery, Heather. *First Thousand Words in Polish.*
London: Usborne Books, 2008.

Hippocrene Polish Children's Picture Dictionary.
New York: Hippocrene Books, 2006.

Turhan, Sedat. *Milet Picture Dictionary: English-Polish.*
London: Milet Publishing, 2005.

Internet Sites

FactHound offers a safe, fun way to find Internet sites related to this book. All of the sites on FactHound have been researched by our staff.

Here's all you do:

Visit *www.facthound.com*

Type in this code: 9781429659642

Super-cool stuff!

Check out projects, games and lots more at
www.capstonekids.com

A+ Books are published by Capstone Press,
151 Good Counsel Drive, P.O. Box 669, Mankato, Minnesota 56002.
www.capstonepub.com

Books published by Capstone Press are manufactured with paper
containing at least 10 percent post-consumer waste.

Library of Congress Cataloging-in-Publication Data
Kudela, Katy R.
    My first book of Polish words / by Katy R. Kudela.
    p. cm. — (A+ Books, Bilingual picture dictionaries)
    Includes bibliographical references.
    Summary: "Simple text paired with themed photos invite the reader to learn to speak Polish"–
Provided by publisher.
    ISBN 978-1-4296-5964-2 (library binding)
    ISBN 978-1-4296-6167-6 (paperback)
    1. Picture dictionaries, Polish. 2. Picture dictionaries, English. 3. Polish language—Dictionaries,
Juvenile—English. 4. English language—Dictionaries, Juvenile–Polish. I. Title. II. Series.
PG6129.E5K83 2011
491.8'5321—dc22   2010029473

Credits
Lori Bye, designer; Wanda Winch, media researcher; Eric Manske, production specialist

Photo Credits
Capstone Studio/Gary Sundermeyer, cover (pig), 20 (farmer with tractor, pig)
Capstone Studio/Karon Dubke, cover (ball, sock), 1, 3, 4–5, 6–7, 8–9, 10–11, 12–13, 14–15,
    16–17, 18–19, 22–23, 24–25, 26–27
Image Farm, back cover, 1, 2, 31, 32 (design elements)
iStockphoto/Andrew Gentry, 28 (main street)
Photodisc, cover (flower)
Shutterstock/Adrian Matthiassen, cover (butterfly); David Hughes, 20 (hay); Eric Isselee,
    20–21 (horse); hamurishi, 28 (bike); Ievgeniia Tikhonova, 21 (chickens); Jim Mills, 29
    (stop sign); Kelli Westfal, 28 (traffic light); Margo Harrison, 20 (sheep); MaxPhoto, 21
    (cow and calf); Melinda Fawver, 29 (bus); Robert Elias, 20–21 (barn, fence); Vladimir
    Mucibabic, 28–29 (city skyline)

Note to Parents, Teachers, and Librarians
Learning to speak a second language at a young age has been shown to improve overall
academic performance, boost problem-solving ability, and foster an appreciation for other
cultures. Early exposure to language skills provides a strong foundation for other subject
areas, including math and reasoning. Introducing children to a second language can help
to lay the groundwork for future academic success and cultural awareness.

Printed in the United States of America in North Mankato, Minnesota.
092010   005933CGS11